MY
FUNNY
FACE
BOOK

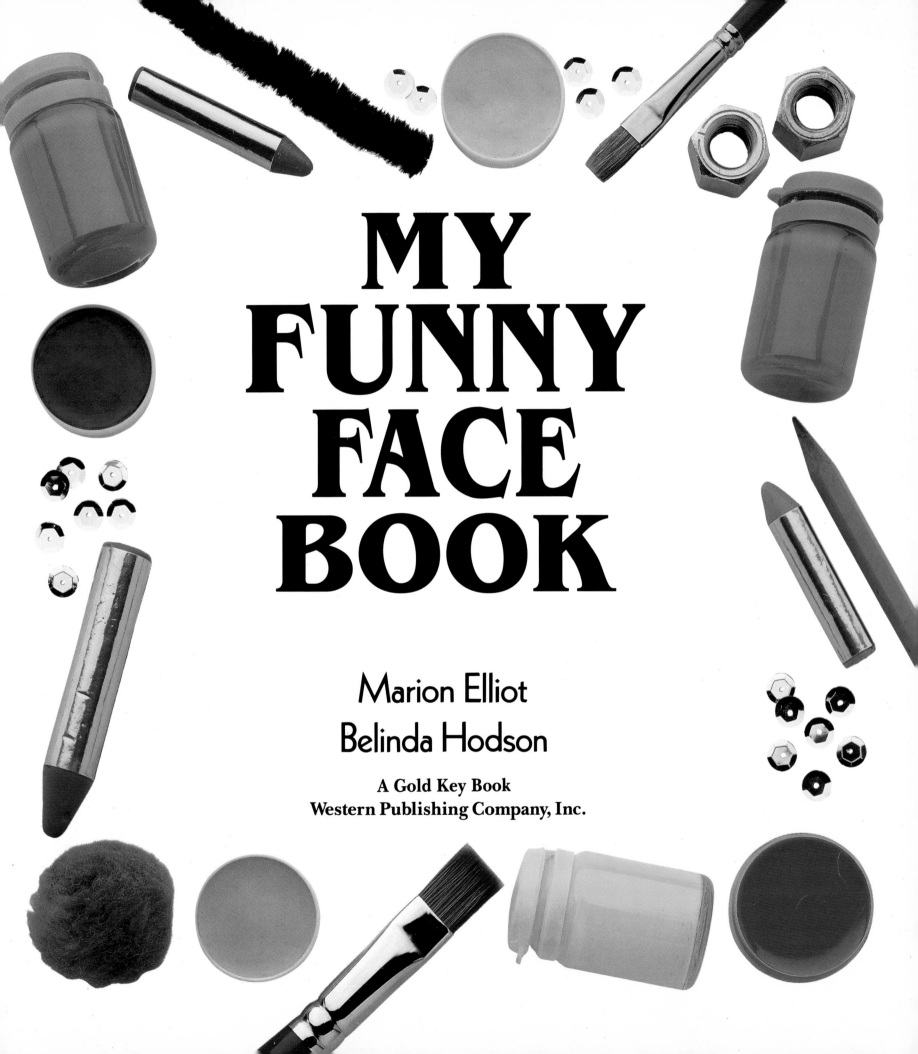

MY FUNNY FACE BOOK

Marion Elliot

Belinda Hodson

A Gold Key Book
Western Publishing Company, Inc.

CONTENTS

INTRODUCTION

My Funny Face Book will show you lots of great ideas to turn yourself into someone else! You will see a wide variety of face painting designs, each with a matching piece of headgear to complete the look.

Ideal for Halloween, costume parties, or performing camp or school plays, these designs can be created with readily available face paints and crayons. The hats and headbands are easily made from cardboard, fabric, or odds and ends found around the house.

Get everything ready before you start, and don't forget to clean up afterward!

Remember to check with an adult before you begin any project; you may need some help.

HOW TO USE THIS BOOK
Each complete look appears on four pages. On the first two pages, you will find an exciting face painting design. On the next two pages are instructions for making the matching hat or headband.

BEFORE YOU BEGIN
- Check with an adult before painting your face. It takes time to apply the paints and remove them. Do you really have enough time or are you supposed to be in bed in 10 minutes?
- Read the instructions before you start and gather together everything you need first.
- When making the hats, cover the work surface with a newspaper or an old cloth.
- Protect your clothes with an apron or wear very old clothes.

WHEN YOU HAVE FINISHED
- Put back the tops on the face paints and wash the paintbrushes and sponges.
- Clean your face properly. Today's face paints are easily removed with soap and water. However, you might like to use a simple cleansing cream as well.
- Put back the tops on any glue or pens that you have used for the hats.
- Put everything away. Store face painting items in old ice-cream containers or cookie tins.

MATERIALS AND EQUIPMENT
For the face designs you will need a variety of face paints. These are now widely available in art supply and toy stores, stationery and department stores, as well as costume or party shops.

When applying makeup, protect your clothes with an apron or cover up with an old shirt.

USING PATTERNS

At the back of the book, you will find patterns for some of the projects. Using a pencil, trace the pattern you need onto tracing paper. If you are making a project with fabric, cut out the pattern and pin it onto the fabric. Cut out the shape. If you want to cut the pattern out of poster board or construction paper, turn your tracing over, lay it on the back of the poster board or construction paper, and rub firmly over the pattern outline with a pencil. The pattern will transfer onto the firm paper. Cut out this shape.

Once you have gained confidence with the designs in this book, go on to adapt the ideas to create your own. Try making up your own face and hat designs.

SAFETY FIRST!

You will be able to make most of the hats and headbands in this book yourself. However, some of the designs use needles or wire. These projects have been marked with a SAFETY TIP. Use common sense when using anything sharp and ask an adult for help.

PLEASE REMEMBER THE BASIC RULES OF SAFETY

- Never leave scissors open or lying around where smaller children can reach them.
- Always stick needles and pins into a pincushion or a scrap of cloth when you are not using them.
- Never use sharp wire without the help or supervision of an adult.

ADULTS TAKE NOTE

Every project in *My Funny Face Book* has been designed for children to paint and make themselves. Occasionally, the headgear projects will require using scissors. Your involvement will depend on the age and ability of the child. You might also like to help with the more advanced face designs. We do recommend that you read through any project before it is undertaken.

The paints come in pots, crayons, or tubes, and almost all can be removed easily with soap and water. Cold cream or a simple cleansing cream will remove any stubborn marks. You can apply the paints with a fingertip, although cosmetic brushes and sponges are easier to use and are also needed for painting in details. These can be bought at variety or drug stores. New paintbrushes can also be used.

The hats and headbands are made from scraps of cardboard, paper, fabric, and pipe cleaners. Most of the items can be bought in stationery or fabric stores or even found around the house. Polystyrene balls and jumbo pipe cleaners are sold in craft or hobby shops.

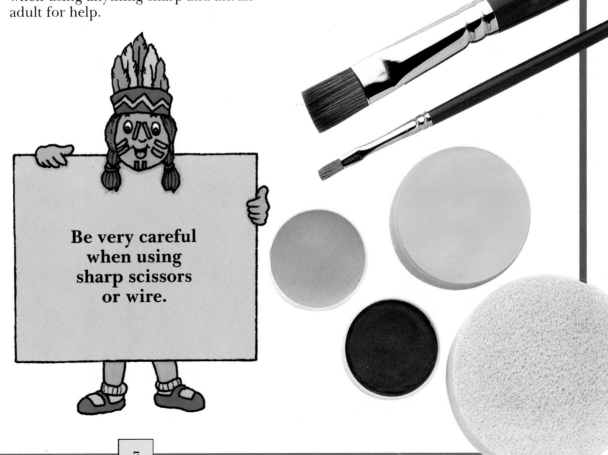

Be very careful when using sharp scissors or wire.

INDIAN CHIEF . . .

Imitate the designs of the Native Americans, whose painted faces were once a surprise to the first settlers. Details of how to make the chief's splendid headdress are shown on the next pages.

1 Dip the sponge into a little water and squeeze it out. Dip the sponge into the tan paint and color your entire face to give it a sunburned look.

2 Using the thick brush, carefully paint green lines on the chin, cheeks, and nose.

YOU WILL NEED

Cosmetic sponge
Dark tan face
   paint
Thick and fine
   paintbrushes
Green face paint
Red face-paint crayon
Red face paint
White face paint

3 Draw lines on both sides of the green stripes using the red crayon.

4 Using the fine brush, paint zigzag lines on top of the green marks you have made on the cheeks. Add a white stripe down the center of the green line on your nose.

...CHIEF'S HEADDRESS

The stunning headdress of the Native American chief was made from cascades of bright feathers that sometimes almost reached the ground. This one is made from colored paper. You can make it as long as you like.

1 Using a pencil and ruler, enlarge the headdress shape on page 56 onto scrap cardboard to make a pattern. Cut it out. Lay the pattern on the red paper and draw around it. Carefully cut out the headdress.

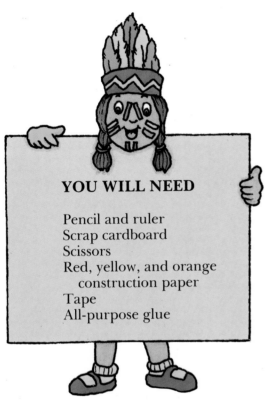

YOU WILL NEED

Pencil and ruler
Scrap cardboard
Scissors
Red, yellow, and orange
   construction paper
Tape
All-purpose glue

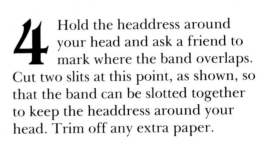

4 Hold the headdress around your head and ask a friend to mark where the band overlaps. Cut two slits at this point, as shown, so that the band can be slotted together to keep the headdress around your head. Trim off any extra paper.

3 Cut out a rectangle of orange paper measuring 10 inches by 3 inches. Glue this to the front of the headband, as shown. Now add a contrasting zigzag band cut from yellow paper. Cut out other decorations and glue them in place.

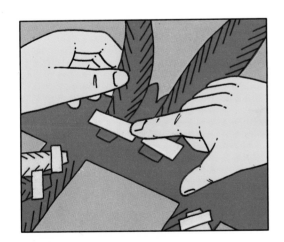

2 Cut a fringe along the inner edge of the two front feathers. Using the picture here as a guide, cut out feather shapes from the red and yellow paper and tape them to the headdress, as shown. For a good effect, alternate the colors of the "feathers."

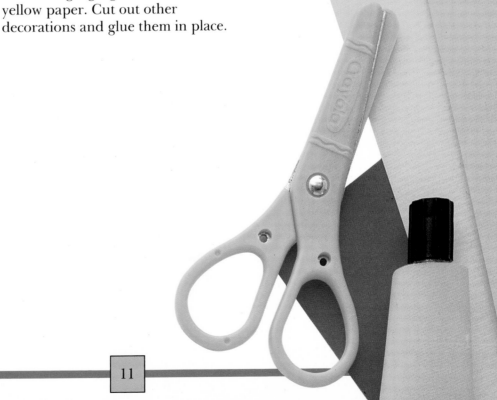

COLORFUL COCKATOO . . .

Paint your face to look like exotic feathers with a bold beak on your nose and mouth. The painting is not difficult if you follow the steps carefully. See how to make a crest of feathers on the next pages.

1 Following the illustration, paint two black oval shapes over your nose and mouth. Paint a border of yellow around the black, as shown. Draw in two little nostrils on the bridge of your nose with the black crayon.

2 Paint green feathers on both cheeks, making a feathery edge toward your hairline. Fill in your cheeks with yellow, blending this into the green for a natural look.

3 Continue painting a feathery pattern up onto your forehead, following the illustration above.

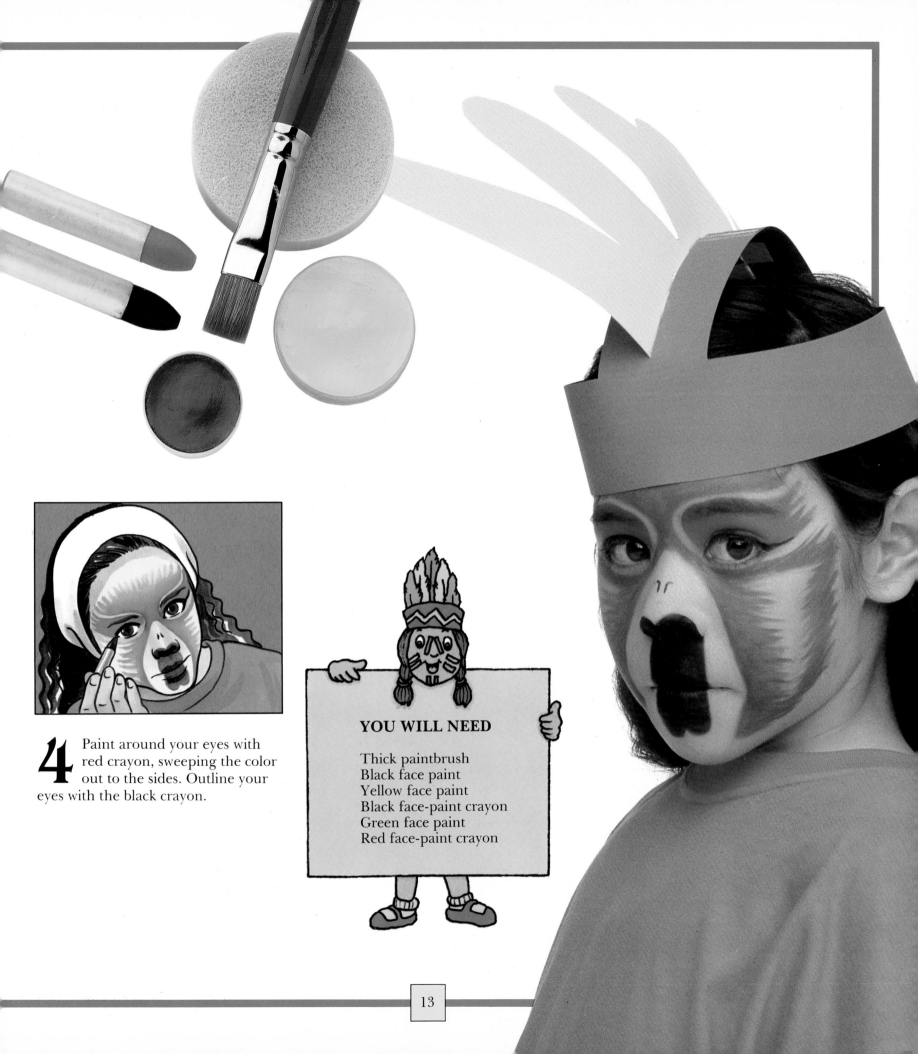

4 Paint around your eyes with red crayon, sweeping the color out to the sides. Outline your eyes with the black crayon.

YOU WILL NEED

Thick paintbrush
Black face paint
Yellow face paint
Black face-paint crayon
Green face paint
Red face-paint crayon

...COCKATOO'S CREST

Cockatoos have magnificent feathered crests on top of their heads. You can make a stunning decorative crest like this, using just one color for the feathers.

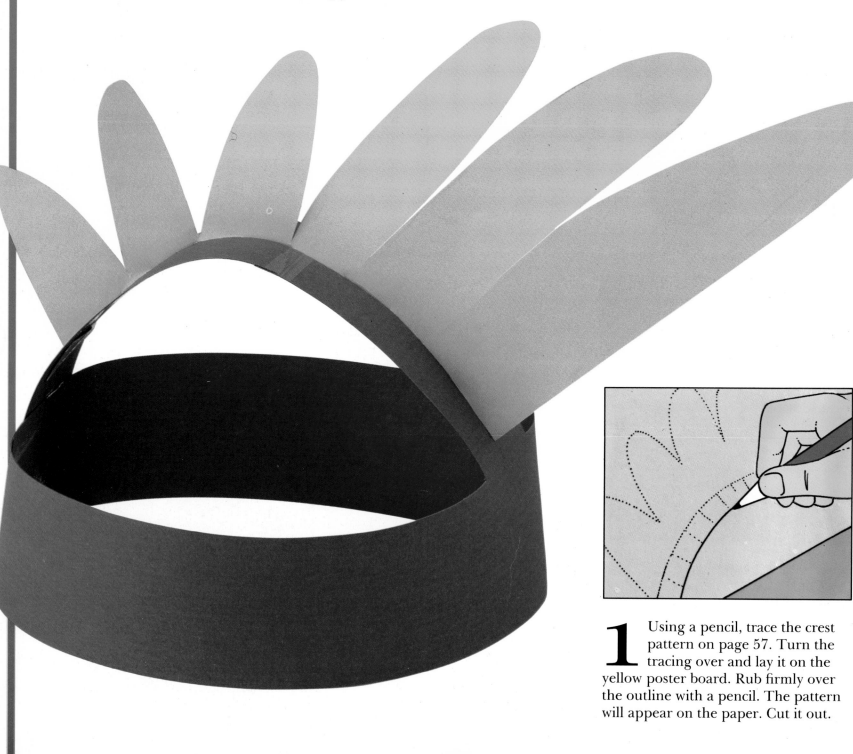

1 Using a pencil, trace the crest pattern on page 57. Turn the tracing over and lay it on the yellow poster board. Rub firmly over the outline with a pencil. The pattern will appear on the paper. Cut it out.

YOU WILL NEED

Pencil and ruler
Tracing paper
Thin yellow and green
   poster board
Scissors
Tape

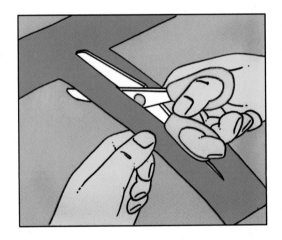

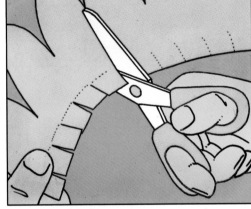

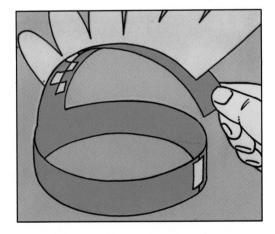

2 Following the pattern on page 57, draw a T shape onto the green poster board using a ruler. Draw a line down the center of the vertical piece. Cut a slit 7 inches long in the middle of the line, as shown.

3 To add the crest, clip along the curved edge to form tabs. Insert the crest into the slit on the headband and bend back each tab back and forth, to the left and right. Secure each tab with a piece of tape.

4 Fit the band around your head. Ask a friend to mark where the band overlaps and tape it together at this point. Bring the crest over your head and tape the loose end to where the band was joined.

GIANT PANDA . . .

In the wild, giant pandas have become more and more rare as their natural habitat has been destroyed. Learn more about this endangered animal before you create your adorable costume.

YOU WILL NEED

Cosmetic sponge
White face paint
Black face paint
Fine paintbrush
Black face-paint crayon
Dark gray face paint

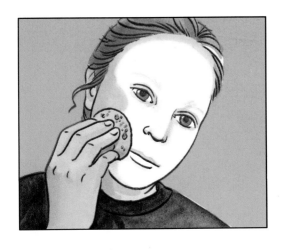

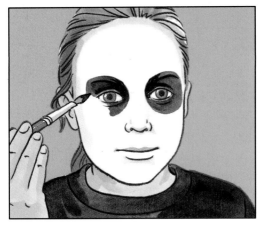

1 Dip the sponge in a little water and squeeze it out. Dip the sponge into the white paint and color your whole face.

2 To create the panda eyes, use the black paint and paintbrush. Carefully paint two large circles around your own eyes.

3 Using the black crayon, draw in the nose and mouth. Follow the illustration as a guide.

4 Give your face a realistic furry look by painting feathery strokes across your face with dark gray paint. This will also soften the white background.

...PANDA EARS

This appealing hat tops your panda face. It is made from fluffy fun fur and is easy to sew. You only need a little of the black fur, so you might even be able to find a scrap in a fabric shop's remnant box.

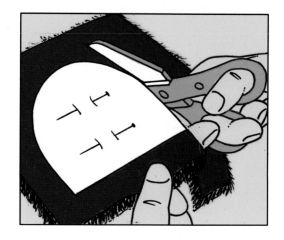

1 Using a pencil, trace the ear pattern on page 57. Cut it out. Pin it to the back of the black fur. Cut out four ear pieces. Make sure that each piece is cut with the fur pile running in the same direction.

YOU WILL NEED

Pencil
Tracing paper
Scissors
Pins
Black fur fabric
White fur fabric
Needle
Black thread
White thread
Press-and-close
   fastening

SAFETY TIP: *Make sure an adult helps you when using a needle.*

2 Cut out a rectangle 22 inches by 7 inches from the white fur. Fold the fabric in half lengthways, right-sides together. Pin along the edges, leaving an 8-inch opening along the top, in the center. Pin two ear shapes right-sides together to make each ear.

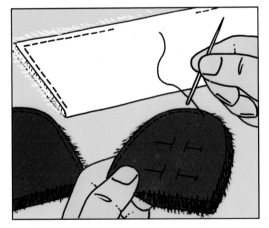

3 Sew the ear pieces together using running stitches, leaving the bottoms open. Sew the side and top seams of the hat band, leaving the 8-inch gap open. Turn the hat band and the ear pieces right-side out.

4 Pin the ears in the opening at the top of the headband. Sew the opening closed, stitching the ears in place as you go. You may want to fold in the raw edge of the fabric as you sew to give a neat finish.

5 At both ends of the band, sew on a strip of press-and-close fastening so the headband fits comfortably around your head.

RUN RABBIT RUN . . .

Follow these instructions for a really professional bunny face—and don't forget the goofy teeth! Every rabbit needs a pair of ears, and these are easy to make. Find out how by turning the page.

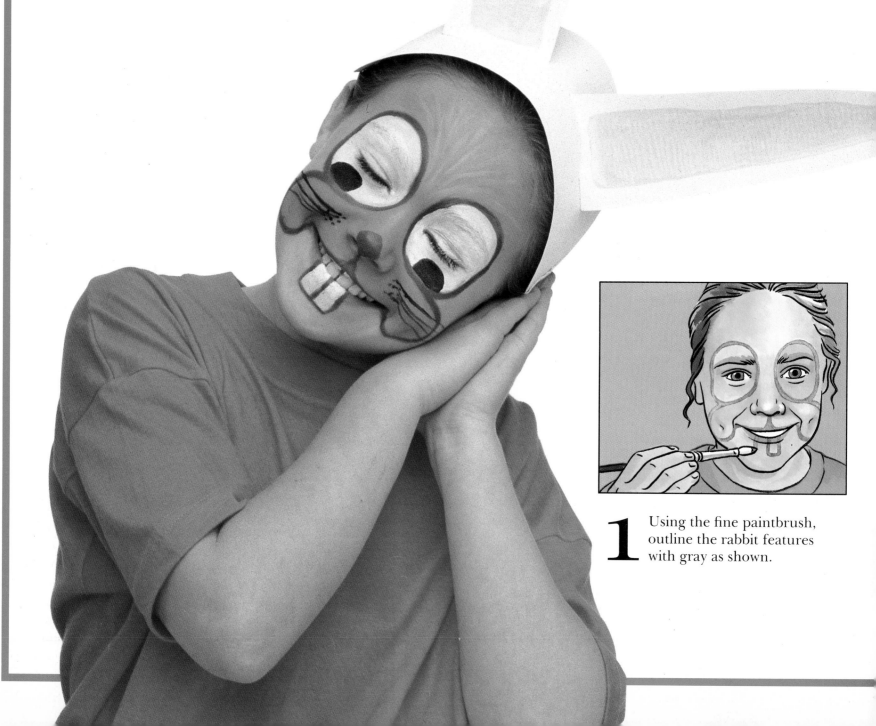

1 Using the fine paintbrush, outline the rabbit features with gray as shown.

2 Change to the thick paintbrush and paint the rest of your face pink. To create a furry effect, paint white feathery strokes on top of the pink, as shown.

3 Fill in the eyes and teeth with white face paint, using the fine brush for the teeth. Color in a bunny nose using gray face paint.

4 Paint in two black eyes with the black face paint. Use the black crayon for some whiskers that sweep across your cheeks.

YOU WILL NEED

Thick and fine
  paintbrushes
Gray face paint
Pink face paint
White face paint
Black face paint
Black face-paint crayon

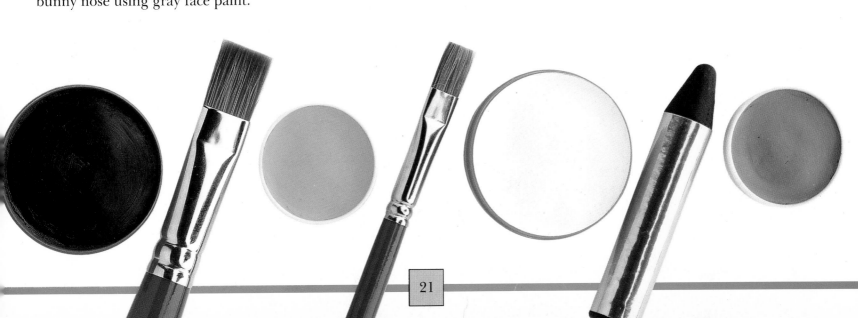

...BUNNY HOP

These easy-to-make bunny ears will complete your rabbit outfit. If you don't use thin poster board, make sure your paper is heavy enough to stand up!

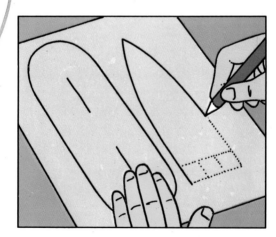

SAFETY TIP: *Make sure an adult helps you when using a needle.*

1 Using a pencil, trace the ear and headband patterns on page 58. Turn the tracings over and lay them on the white poster board. Rub firmly over the outlines with a pencil. The patterns will appear on the poster board. Cut out each piece. Remember to make two ears!

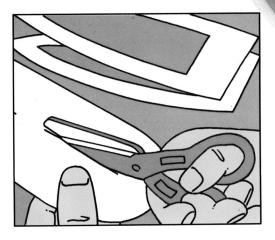

2 Paint in the pink area on each ear. Cut two slits in the headband, as shown on the pattern.

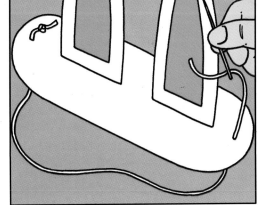

4 Ask an adult to help you make a hole at each end of the headband with a darning needle. Thread the elastic through the holes and adjust the hat so that it fits comfortably. Make a knot at both ends of the elastic.

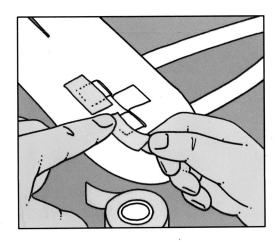

3 Make two cuts into the base of each ear along the marks on the pattern to form tabs. Insert each ear in the headband. Open out the tabs. Tape the tabs to the back of the headband, as shown.

YOU WILL NEED

Pencil
Tracing paper
Thin white poster board
Paintbrush
Pink poster paint
Scissors
Tape
Darning needle
Thin elastic

ROCKET MAN . . .

Become an intergalactic traveler or alien from outer space. It's fun to decorate your face with planets and spaceships, although it takes concentration and a steady hand. Find out how to make the rocket man's headgear on the next pages.

1 With the thick brush, paint a yellow circle around one eye to represent the moon.

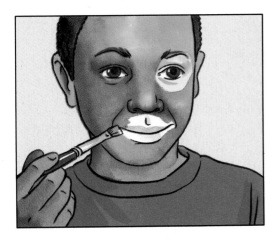

2 Outline a large spaceship across your mouth using the fine paintbrush and the silver paint. Fill in the outline with silver using the thick brush.

3 On one cheek, use the fine brush to paint another smaller spaceship in silver. Paint little black dots across the spaceships to look like windows.

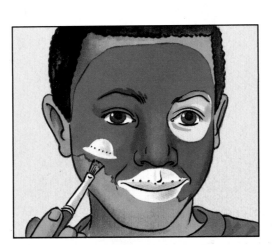

4 Color the rest of your face dark blue. Use the fine brush to paint around the moon and spaceships. You can add glitter if you want to add a sparkly, starry effect.

YOU WILL NEED

Thick and fine
  paintbrushes
Yellow face paint
Silver face paint
Black face paint
Dark blue face paint
Glitter

...RACE TO SPACE

Complete your intergalactic look with this rocket-and-planets headband. The planets are made from polystyrene balls which are available in various sizes from craft and hobby shops.

1 Trace the rocket and star patterns on page 59. Cut them out. Pin each pattern to different colored felt and cut out two of each piece, as shown.

SAFETY TIP: *Make sure an adult helps you when using wire.*

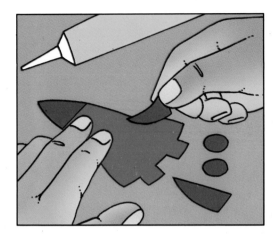

2 Glue small pieces of felt onto one side of each rocket shape for decoration.

YOU WILL NEED

Pencil
Tracing paper
Scissors
Pins
Scraps of felt in
    different colors
All-purpose glue
Four 8-inch
    lengths of thread-
    covered wire
Thick paintbrush
Poster paints
Two polystyrene balls
Headband

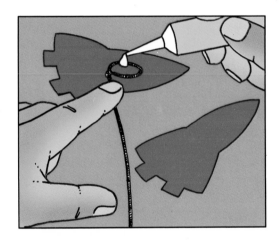

3 Take one piece of wire and bend one end into a loop. Put the loop on the back of one rocket shape and secure it with a little glue. Stick a second rocket shape on top to cover the wire. Repeat this step for the star shape.

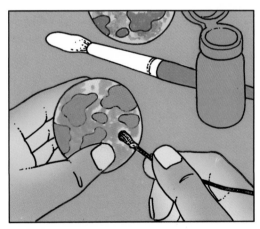

4 Paint each polystyrene ball to look like a planet. Ask an adult to help you make a hole in the base of each one using the wire. Drip some glue into the holes. Make a small loop at the end of each length of wire and push a loop into each hole. Let the glue dry.

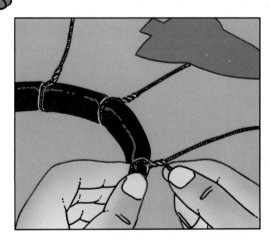

5 Attach the outer space shapes to the headband by twisting the free end of each piece of wire tightly around it. Ask an adult to help make sure that there are no loose ends of wire that could scratch you.

CLOWNING AROUND...

It's circus time with this happy clown face. Why not get together with a few friends and give a show with juggling and tricks? You might even try to train your pets for an animal act!

YOU WILL NEED

Cosmetic sponge
White face paint
Thick and fine paintbrushes
Blue face paint
Green face-paint crayon
Red face-paint crayon
Red face paint

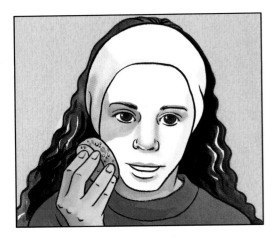

1 Dip the sponge into a little water and squeeze it out. Dip the sponge into the white paint and color your whole face.

3 Using the red crayon, outline a big, happy mouth like the one shown here. Fill it in with red paint using the thick brush. On the bottom lip, paint two white teeth.

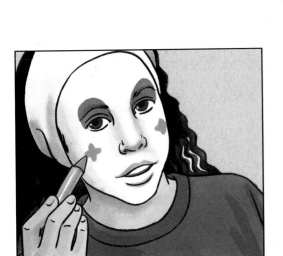

2 Using the fine brush, paint a blue oval above each eye. On each cheek, draw a green cross with the crayon.

4 Using the red paint or crayon, paint a circle on your nose. Finish off with white highlights painted on your nose and mouth.

...THE BIG TOP

This festive hat with its bright pom-poms is easy to make and completes your circus face. You can buy ready-made pom-poms from craft shops, or make your own from scraps of wool.

1 On a large piece of thin cardboard measuring at least 12 inches deep, draw a straight vertical line 12 inches in from the end, as shown, to form a square.

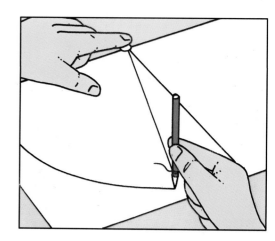

2 Tie one end of a piece of string to a thumbtack. Now tie a pencil to the string 12 inches away from the thumbtack. Press the thumbtack into the cardboard at the top of the vertical line. Draw a curve from the top left corner to the bottom of the vertical line.

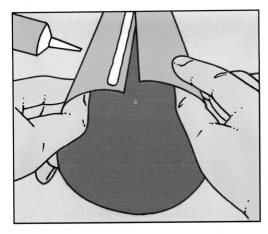

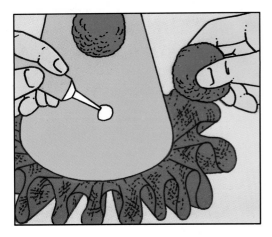

3 Cut out the shape you have drawn. Lay the shape on the crepe paper. Draw around it, allowing one extra inch all around. Cut this out.

4 Fold the edges of the crepe paper over onto the cardboard, holding them with glue. Bring the two straight edges together to form a cone. Glue them in place.

5 Cut a piece of red net about 3 inches wide and long enough to go around the base of the hat twice. Gather the net loosely along the long edge with long running stitches so that it fits inside the brim. Using tape, stick the net on to the inside edge of the brim. Decorate the hat with pom-poms.

SAFETY TIP: *Make sure an adult helps you when using a needle.*

YOU WILL NEED

Thin cardboard
Pencil and ruler
String
Thumbtack
Scissors
Yellow crepe paper
All-purpose glue
Red net
Needle and thread
Four pom-poms
Tape

UNDER THE SEA . . .

This jaunty boat sits on top of your head, unaware of the octopus lurking just below the surface! Although this design needs concentration and a steady hand, it is lots of fun to paint.

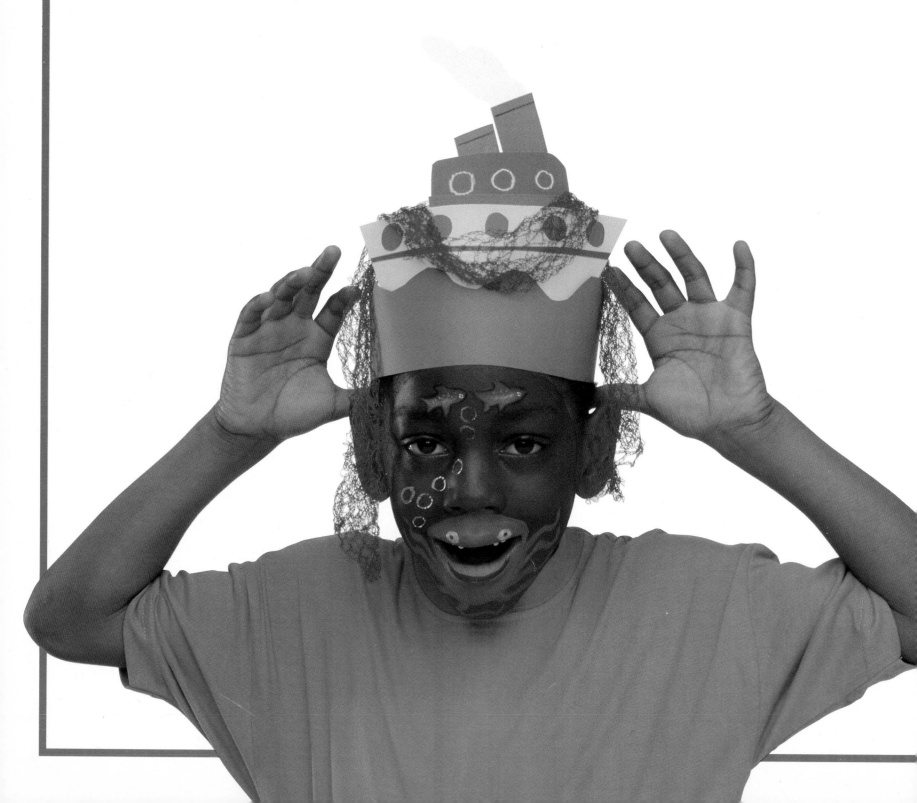

1 With a fine paintbrush, draw in the outline of the octopus in pink. For the best effect, draw the outline over your mouth and down your chin, as shown.

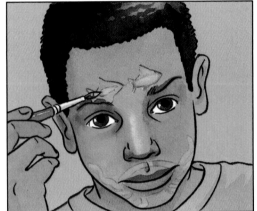

2 Using green and yellow face paint, add two fish swimming across your forehead.

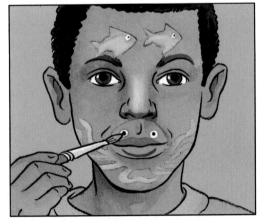

3 Fill in the octopus with pink paint. Put in white eyes and add black dots. Do the same to the fish.

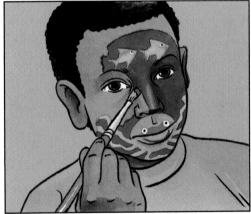

4 Carefully fill in the rest of your face with blue paint to look like the sea. Use a fine brush to paint around the octopus and fish. Add a few bubbles up one cheek with white paint.

YOU WILL NEED

Thick and fine paintbrushes
Pink, green, yellow, white, blue, and black face paints

...ABOVE THE WAVES

Complete your nautical scene with this buoyant little boat. It's very colorful, and the fishing net was once a bag that held oranges.

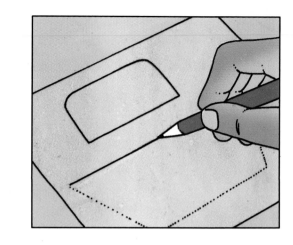

1 Using a pencil, trace the body and cabin patterns on page 59. Turn the tracings over and lay them on the colored poster board. Rub firmly over the outlines with a pencil. The patterns will appear on the poster board. Cut out each piece.

2 Cut out two funnels, five portholes, and a puff of white smoke. Glue them to the boat. Draw in extra details with wax crayons.

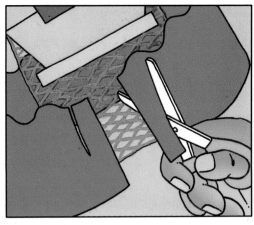

YOU WILL NEED
Pencil and ruler
Tracing paper
Thin poster board in
several colors
Scissors; tape
All-purpose glue
Wax crayons
Net bag

5 Hold the finished hat around your head and ask a friend to mark the point at which the ends overlap. Cut two slits into the band at this point, as shown, so that the band can be slotted together.

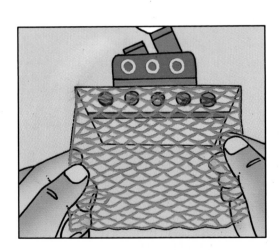

3 For the net, cut along the seam of the net bag and open it out. Arrange the net so that it hangs over the edge of the boat. Hold it in place with tape.

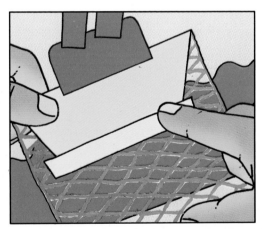

4 For the headband, cut a strip of blue poster board 22 inches by 3 inches, trimming one edge so that it's wavy. Attach the boat to the headband with tape.

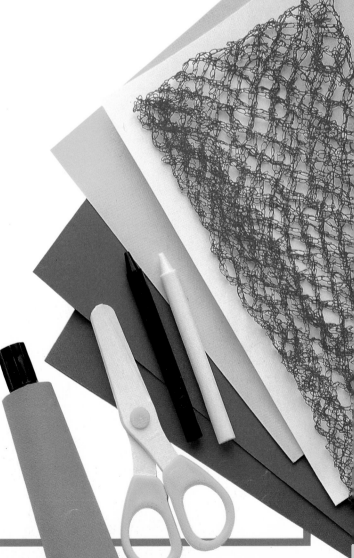

GENTLE GIRAFFE . . .

Most designs from nature are very beautiful. The patches on the skin of the giraffe are wonderful. Imitate these marks on your face and continue them on the wacky headdress, explained on the next pages.

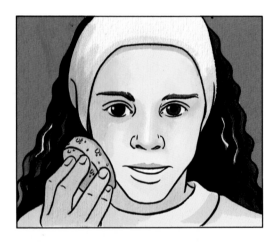

1 Dip the sponge in a little water and squeeze it out. Dip the sponge into the yellow paint and color your whole face.

2 Using the dark brown paint and brush, outline the patches on your face.

YOU WILL NEED

Cosmetic sponge
Yellow face paint
Dark brown face paint
Thick paintbrush
Dark brown face-paint
 crayon
Orange face paint

3 Fill in the patches using the brown crayon or paint. Add some orange paint for a more realistic look.

4 Make your skin look slightly furry by adding feathery strokes around the patches with the dark brown paint.

...DIZZY HEIGHTS

Giraffes are very elegant creatures. Their long necks give them a distinctive look. Match the color of this headdress with your face paint for the best overall effect.

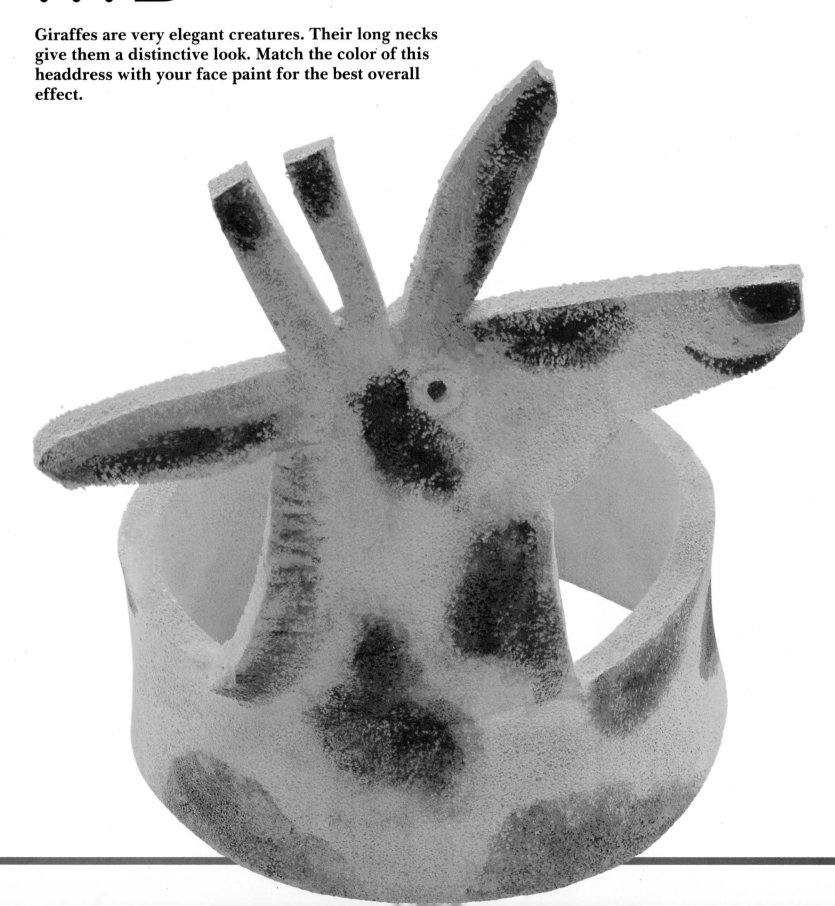

YOU WILL NEED

Pencil and ruler
Tracing paper
Scissors
Masking tape
Foam rubber ½ inch thick
Thick and fine paintbrushes
Brown, yellow, black, and
   white poster paints
Needle and thread or
   all-purpose glue
Press-and-close fastening

SAFETY TIP: *Make sure an adult helps you when using a needle.*

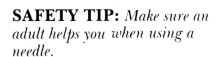

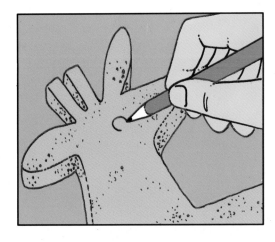

2 Paint the front of the giraffe yellow and let it dry. Draw the features and markings on the giraffe with a soft pencil.

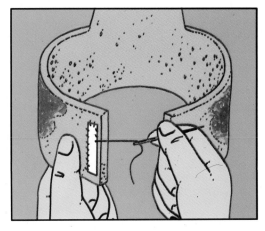

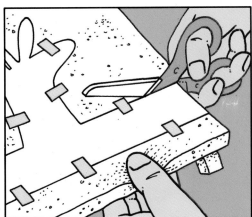

1 Using the pencil, trace the giraffe pattern on page 60. Extend each side by 10 inches from the dotted line. Cut it out. Tape the pattern to the foam rubber. Cut out the foam.

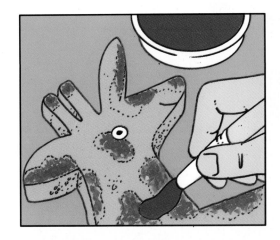

3 Fill in the giraffe's features with poster paints. When the front of the hat is thoroughly dry, turn it over and paint the back yellow.

4 When the paint has dried, hold the hat around your head and ask a friend to mark the point at which the ends overlap. Sew or glue on a strip of press-and-close fastening at this point so the headband fits comfortably around your head.

RATTLING BONES..

Scare the wits out of your family and friends with this ghoulish face and voodoo hat. This face is one of the easiest to paint in the book, using only black and white face paints. Turn the page to find out how to make the hat.

1 Dip the sponge into a little water and squeeze it out. Dip the sponge into the white paint and color your whole face.

2 Using the thick brush, carefully paint two large black circles around your eyes.

YOU WILL NEED

Cosmetic sponge
White face paint
Thick and fine
  paintbrushes
Black face paint
Black face-paint crayon

3 Give your face a skeletal shape by painting a black outline under your chin and beneath your cheekbones. Use the fine brush to paint a triangle on your nose.

4 Turn your mouth into skeletal teeth using the black crayon. Follow the illustration shown as a guide.

...DRY BONES

Make this voodoo hat to go with your skeleton face. Take it one step further and make paper bones to stick to an old black T-shirt to give you a complete Halloween or party costume.

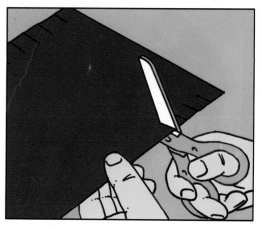

1 To make the hat crown, draw a rectangle 7½ inches by 23 inches onto one sheet of the black poster board using the pencil and ruler. Cut it out and snip along both long sides to make ½-inch tabs, as shown.

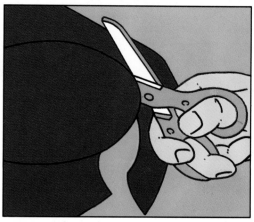

2 Using a pencil, trace the oval hat top pattern on page 61. Turn your tracing over and lay it on the black poster board. Rub firmly over the outline with a pencil. The pattern will appear on the black poster board. Cut it out.

3 Bend the tabs along one edge of the crown. Spread glue around the edge of the hat top and stick the crown to it, bending it around and overlapping the tabs to get a good fit. Glue the edges of the crown together neatly.

5 Fold the tabs on the bottom edge of the hat crown outward. Pull one brim piece down over the crown so that it sits on the tabs. Glue it into place. Glue the other brim piece to the underside of the hat to hide the tabs.

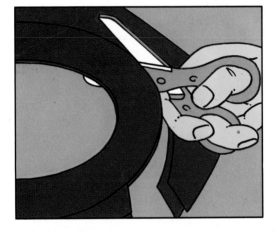

4 Trace the hat brim pattern on page 61. Turn your tracing over and lay it on the other piece of black poster board. Rub firmly over the outline with a pencil. The pattern will appear on the poster board. Either cut the shape from a double thickness of black poster board or cut two separate brim pieces.

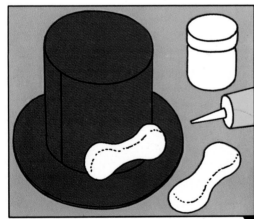

6 Paint the two dog biscuits with several coats of white paint. When they are completely dry, glue them to the front of the hat.

TICKTOCK...

This quick and easy face design is topped with a clever cuckoo clock hat. Ticktock makes a simple, fun costume for a party or contest.

1 Dip the sponge in a little water and squeeze it out. Dip the sponge into the light brown paint and color your whole face.

3 Mark the positions of the numbers in between with little orange lines.

4 Using the paintbrush and the dark brown paint, draw in the two hands of the clock across your nose, as shown.

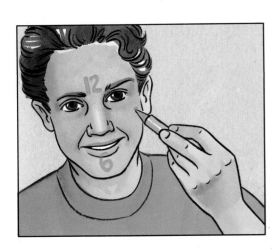

2 Using the orange crayon, write in the numbers. Start with "12" on your forehead, then "6" on your chin, "9" on your right cheek, and "3" on your left cheek.

...CUCKOO CLOCK

This funny hat tops your Ticktock face. Based on a Swiss cuckoo clock, this sweet little bird permanently announces the time for you!

1 Using a pencil and ruler, enlarge the clock body shape on page 63 onto scrap cardboard to make a pattern (see page 56 for how to do this). Cut it out. Lay the pattern on the brown poster board and draw around it. Cut it out.

SAFETY TIP: *Make sure an adult helps you when using wire.*

2 Using a pencil, trace the bird on page 62. Turn the tracing over and lay it on the yellow poster board. Rub firmly over the outline with a pencil. The pattern will appear on the poster board. Cut out the bird. Draw on its features with wax crayons.

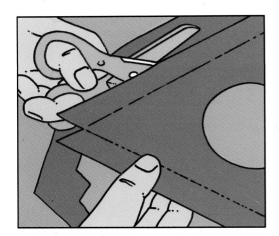

3 Follow Step 2 to trace the clock back and clock front patterns, on page 62, onto the brown poster board. Remember to add the opening to the clock front only. Cut out these pieces and cut out the opening.

4 Curl the wire around your finger to make a coil shape. Tape one end of the wire to the back of the bird and the other to the inside of the clock opening.

5 Using glue, stick the lower edges of the front and back panels to the main clock body, as shown.

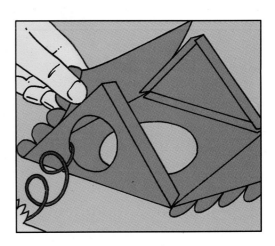

6 Stick the sides of the clock body onto the tabs on the front and back panels. Make sure the glue is completely dry before you try on the hat.

PURR-FECT FELINE . . .

A furry face and hat will turn you into the purr-fect cat. Although the face looks a little difficult, it is quite simple to create a furry effect with brown paint and a thick paintbrush.

YOU WILL NEED

Cosmetic sponge
Medium brown face paint
Mustard-colored face paint
Thick and fine paintbrushes
Dark brown face-paint crayon
White face paint

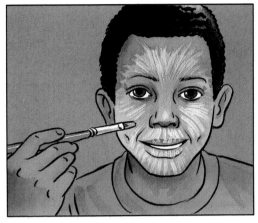

2 Go over your face again, this time using the mustard color and a thick brush. Use light, feathery strokes for the best effect.

4 Fill in the nose with brown paint and add whiskers along your upper lip. Add more feathery strokes, using both white and brown on a brush, to make the fur even more realistic.

1 Dip the sponge in a little water and squeeze it out. Dip it into the brown paint. Using feathery strokes, sponge the paint all over your face, so that it looks like fur.

3 Using the brown crayon, draw in the outlines of the eyes, tip of the nose, and mouth, as shown. Darken the eyebrows, making them more shaggy.

...PURR-FECT FINISH

This hat is the purr-fect finishing touch!
The whiskers are made from an old brush and
the headband is made from fur fabric, usually used
for making soft toys. By adding shaggy fur on the
sides, you could go wild and turn yourself
into a lion.

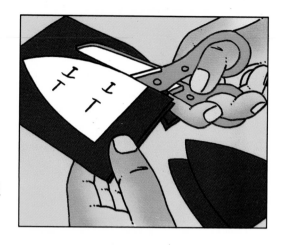

1 Using a pencil, trace the ear pattern on page 63. Cut it out. Pin it onto a double thickness of felt. Cut around the pattern to make two ear pieces. Repeat this to make four ear pieces.

SAFETY TIP: *Make sure an adult helps you when using a needle.*

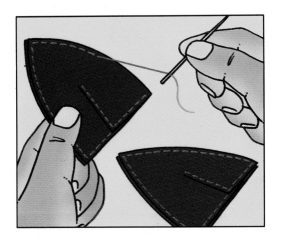

YOU WILL NEED

Pencil
Tracing paper
Scissors
Pins
Brown felt
Needle and thread
Brown fur fabric
Bristles from an old
    brush
Tape
Press-and-close
    fastener

2 Snip a little way up the center of each piece. Overlap the cut edges and sew them together to make a small pleat. Pin two ear pieces together to make each ear. Sew them together with small running stitches. Repeat this for the second ear.

3 Cut out a strip of fur fabric 22 inches by 7 inches. Fold the fabric in half lengthways, right-sides together. Pin along the edges, leaving an 8-inch opening at the top, in the center. Sew the edges, leaving the 8-inch gap open. Turn the hat band right-side out.

4 Pin the ears to one side of the opening. Bind the ends of the bristles with tape and pin them between the ears. Sew everything in place, making sure the stitches don't show through on the right side.

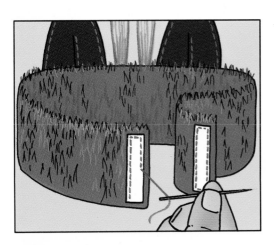

5 Sew the opening closed to cover the ends of the ears and bristles. At both ends of the band, sew on a strip of the press-and-close fastener, adjusting the headband to fit.

COUNT VAMPULA . . .

A perfect disguise for Halloween, this spooky
vampire face will scare even the bravest soul! You can
use water or gel to slick back your hair—the bat-wing
hat (on the next pages) will keep it in place.

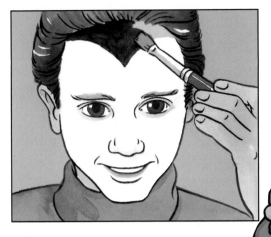

YOU WILL NEED

Hair gel (optional)
Cosmetic sponge
White face paint
Thick paintbrush
Black face paint
Dark gray face paint
Red face-paint crayon

1 Slick back your hair with either gel or water. Use a damp sponge dipped into the white paint to color your face. Paint a V shape or "widow's peak" onto your forehead with the black paint.

2 Using the dark gray paint, lightly color the lids of your eyes and the area underneath. Suck in your cheeks to make two "hollows." Color these in with more dark gray paint.

3 Use the black paint to darken both eyebrows. With the red crayon, paint a line underneath both eyes. Rub the crayon across your lips to redden them.

4 Paint two white fangs onto your mouth and add dripping blood with the red crayon.

...BAT-WING HAT

You'll have a lot of fun creeping around in this spooky bat-wing hat, but remember not to come out before the sun goes down! The basic hat pattern is a good starting point for a variety of designs.

1 Using a pencil, trace the hat and bat-wing patterns on page 63. Cut out the hat pattern. Pin it to a double thickness of black felt. Cut around the pattern to make two hat sections. Repeat the process twice so that you have six pieces of hat.

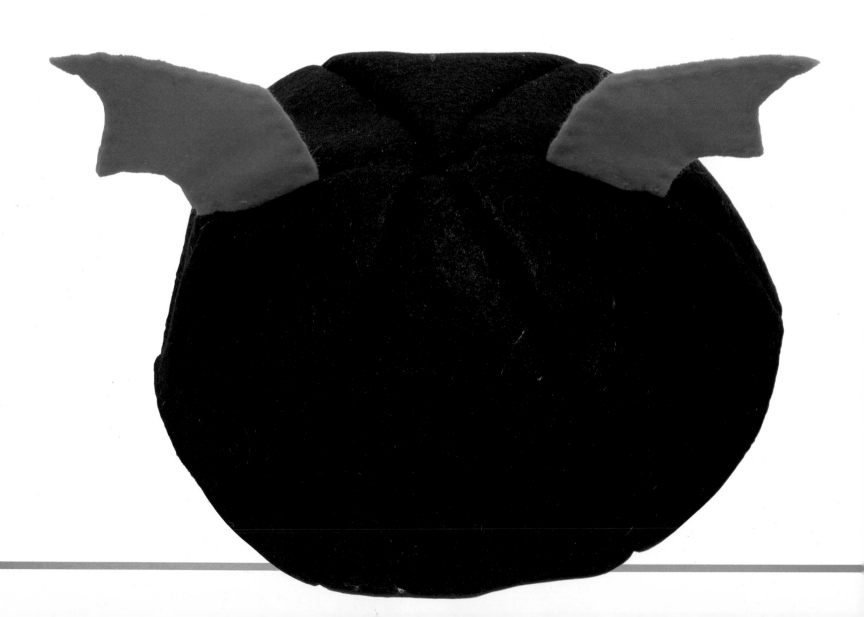

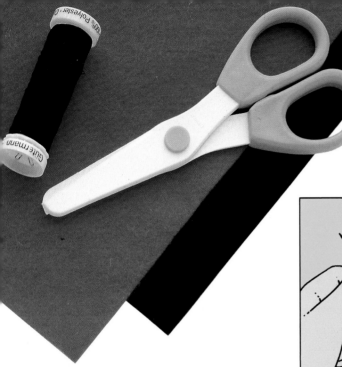

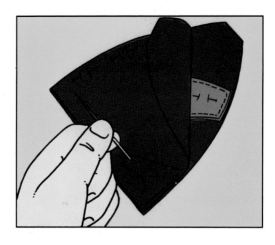

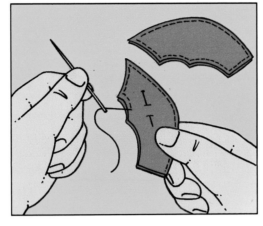

3 Pin two bat-wing pieces together. Sew around the edges with small running stitches. Repeat the process to make the other wing.

4 Take two hat sections and pin a wing section between them, as shown. Pin the sections together. Sew up one side, stitching the bat wing in place as you go. Remove all the pins. Repeat the process for the other wing.

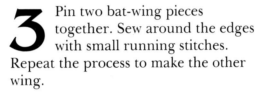

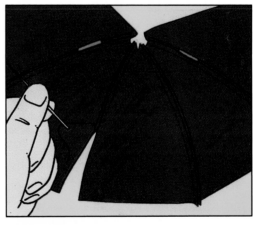

2 Cut out the bat-wing pattern. Pin to a double thickness of red felt. Cut around the pattern to make two wings. Repeat the process so that you have four pieces.

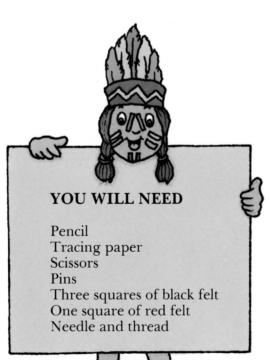

YOU WILL NEED

Pencil
Tracing paper
Scissors
Pins
Three squares of black felt
One square of red felt
Needle and thread

5 Pin and sew the remaining two panels in between the hat and wing sections. Make sure that there are eventually three hat panels between each wing. Trim the side seams slightly. Then turn the hat right-side out.

SAFETY TIP: *Make sure an adult helps you when using a needle.*

PATTERNS

Many of the headpieces in this book are based on the patterns given on the following pages. To find out how to copy a pattern, follow the step-by-step instructions given for each project.

    Some of the patterns are shown as diagrams with measurements. You will need to make your own full-size pattern. To do this, draw the shape onto paper or cardboard, following the measurements. Use a pencil and ruler and start with the longest straight edge. Double-check all measurements before cutting out your pattern.

    The hats are all designed to fit an average 9- to 11-year-old. Most are adjustable, but check at the pattern stage to see if the size is right for you before cutting out the final pieces.

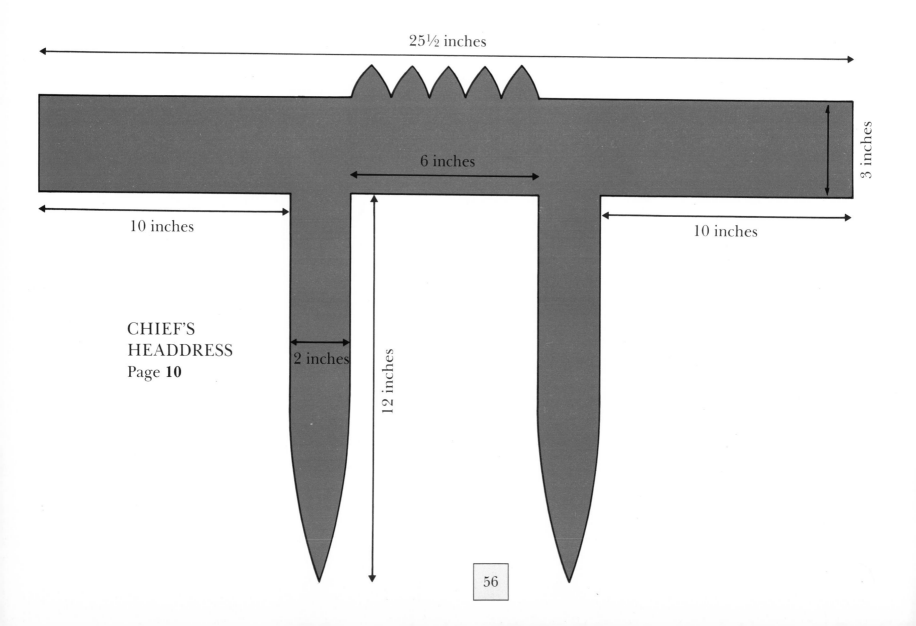

25½ inches

3 inches

6 inches

10 inches

10 inches

CHIEF'S
HEADDRESS
Page **10**

2 inches

12 inches

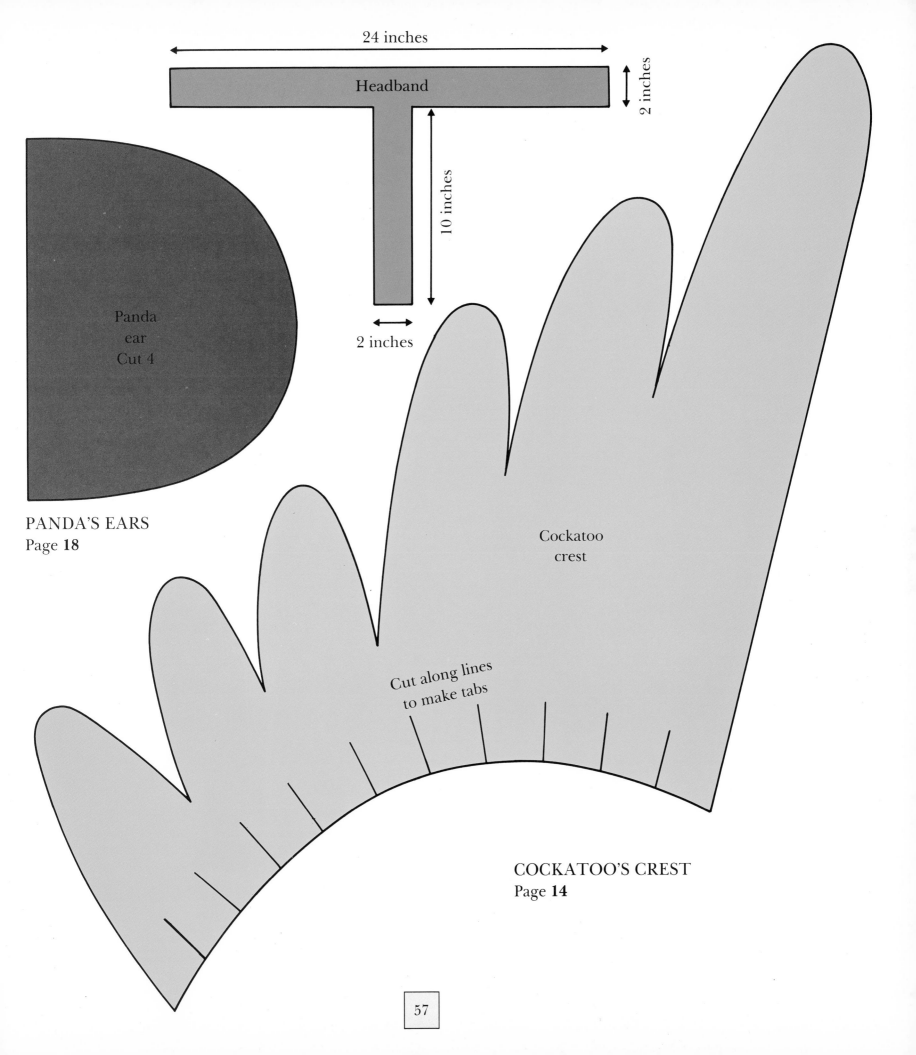

24 inches

Headband

2 inches

10 inches

2 inches

Panda
ear
Cut 4

PANDA'S EARS
Page **18**

Cockatoo
crest

Cut along lines
to make tabs

COCKATOO'S CREST
Page **14**

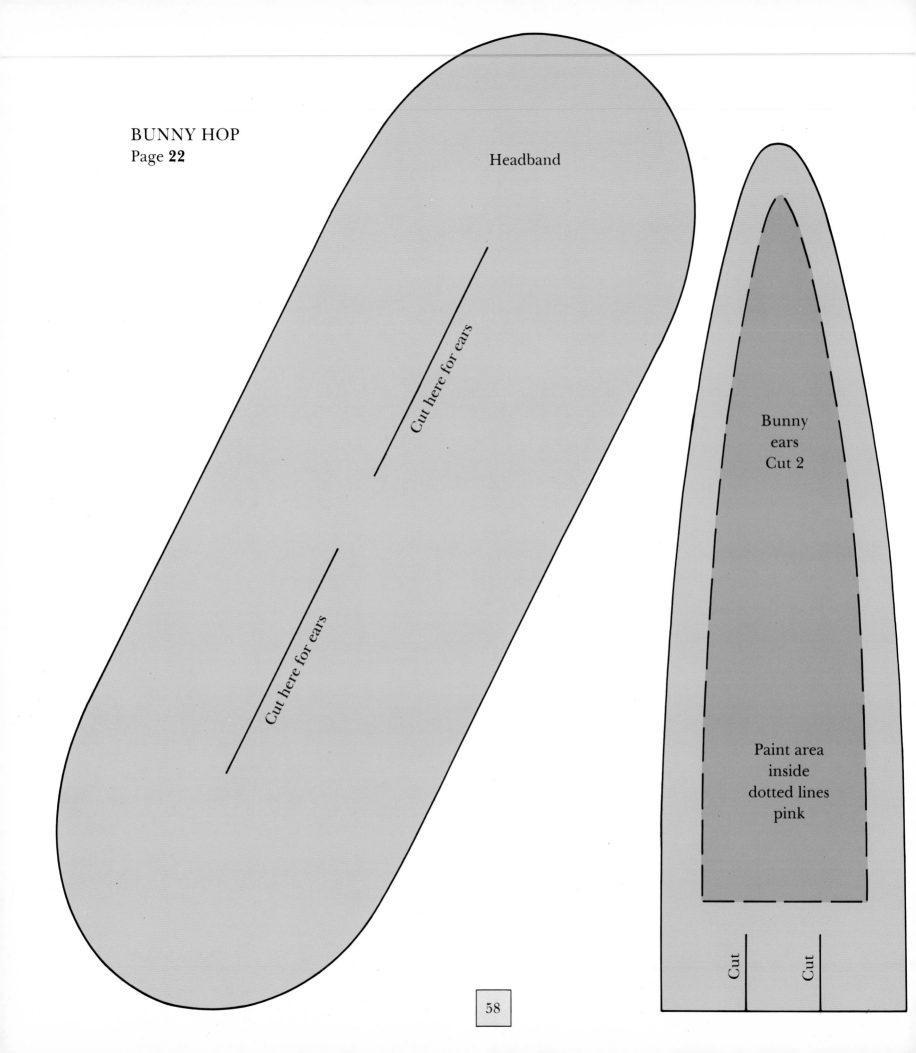

BUNNY HOP
Page **22**

Headband

Cut here for ears

Cut here for ears

Bunny
ears
Cut 2

Paint area
inside
dotted lines
pink

Cut

Cut

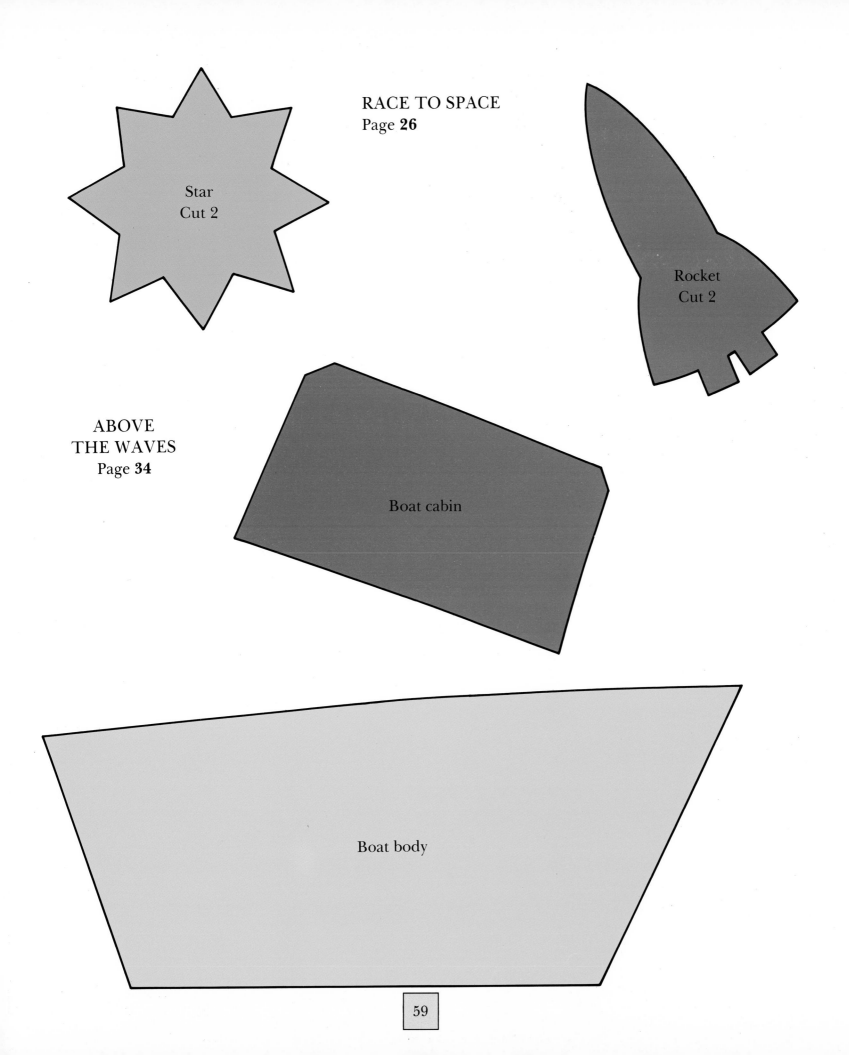

Star
Cut 2

RACE TO SPACE
Page **26**

Rocket
Cut 2

ABOVE
THE WAVES
Page **34**

Boat cabin

Boat body

Giraffe
head

Extend band by 10 inches

Extend band by 10 inches

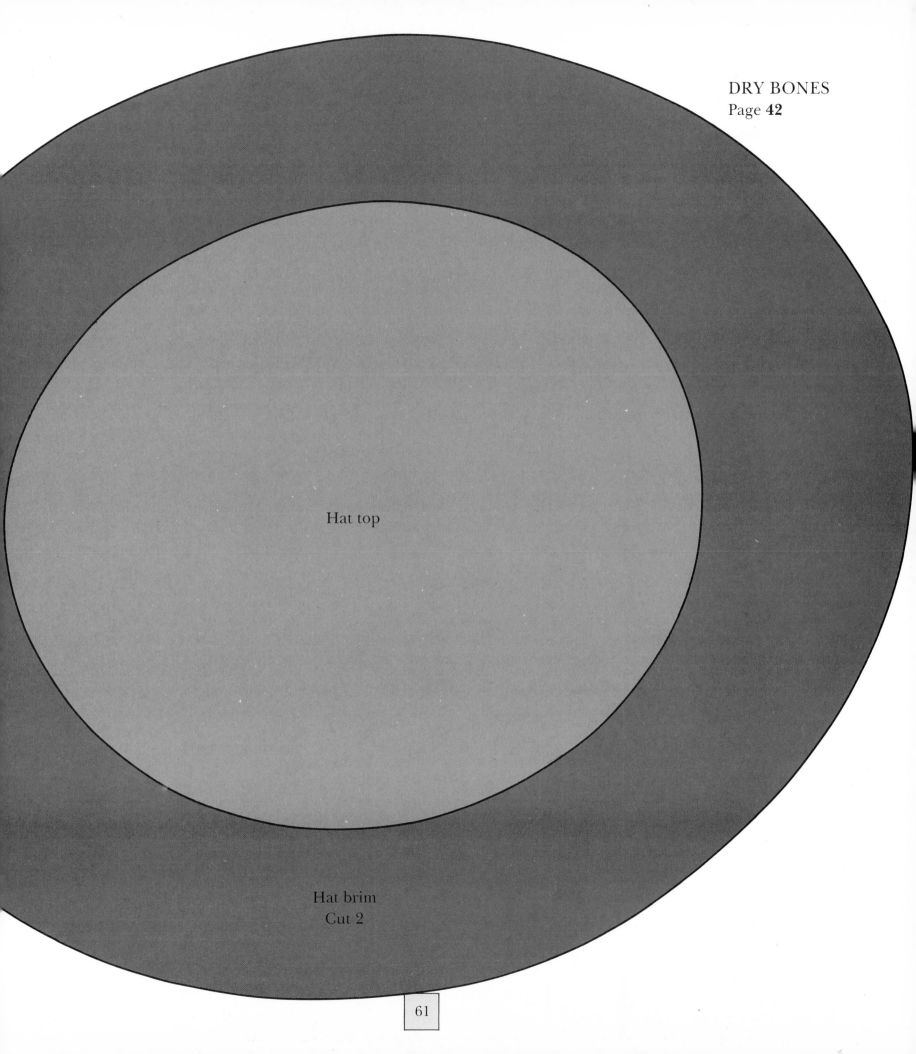

Hat top

Hat brim
Cut 2

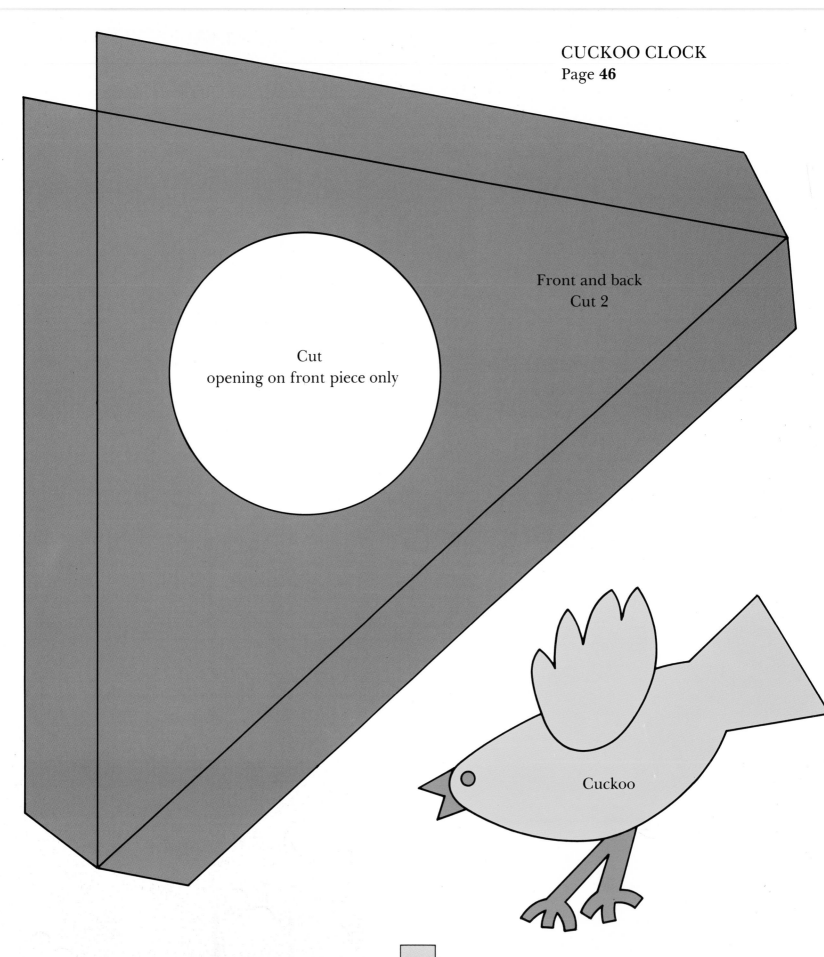

Front and back
Cut 2

Cut
opening on front piece only

Cuckoo

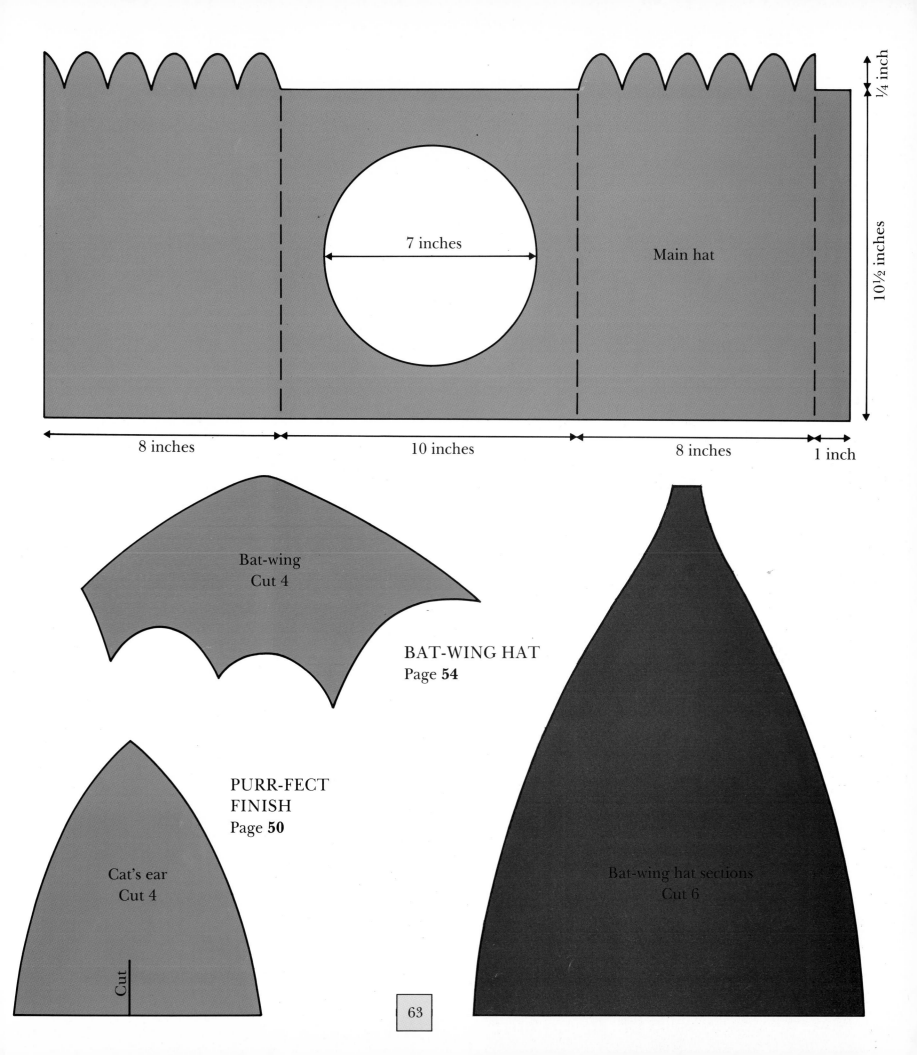

7 inches

Main hat

¼ inch

10½ inches

8 inches

10 inches

8 inches

1 inch

Bat-wing
Cut 4

BAT-WING HAT
Page **54**

PURR-FECT
FINISH
Page **50**

Cat's ear
Cut 4

Cut

Bat-wing hat sections
Cut 6

INDEX

ACKNOWLEDGMENTS
The author and publishers would like to thank Grimas Theatrical Make-up, Lee Lane, Horwich, Bolton BL6 7JD for supplying face paints for this book.

Model Agencies
Rascals, 9 Queen's Road, Buckhurst Hill, Essex IG9 5BZ
Scallywags, 1 Cranbrook Rise, Cranbrook, Ilford, Essex IG1 3QW